I Can Take Care of My Body!

"Healthy Me Series"

Andi Cann

Kids love to take care of themselves…except when they don't! This book encourages children to be independent and self-sufficient by keeping clean and healthy!

Hi, I'm Riley.

Hi, I'm Rae, Riley's sister. We are learning how to take care of our bodies.

Our mom does a great job of taking care of things to keep us healthy! She washes our clothes,

and makes us yummy, healthy food,

and takes us to the doctor to get shots so we don't get sick.

All of these things keep us healthy! But I can take care of myself, too!

Mom says I love myself when I take care of myself!

We have awesome bodies and need to take care of them!

Look at all the parts that make up our bodies.

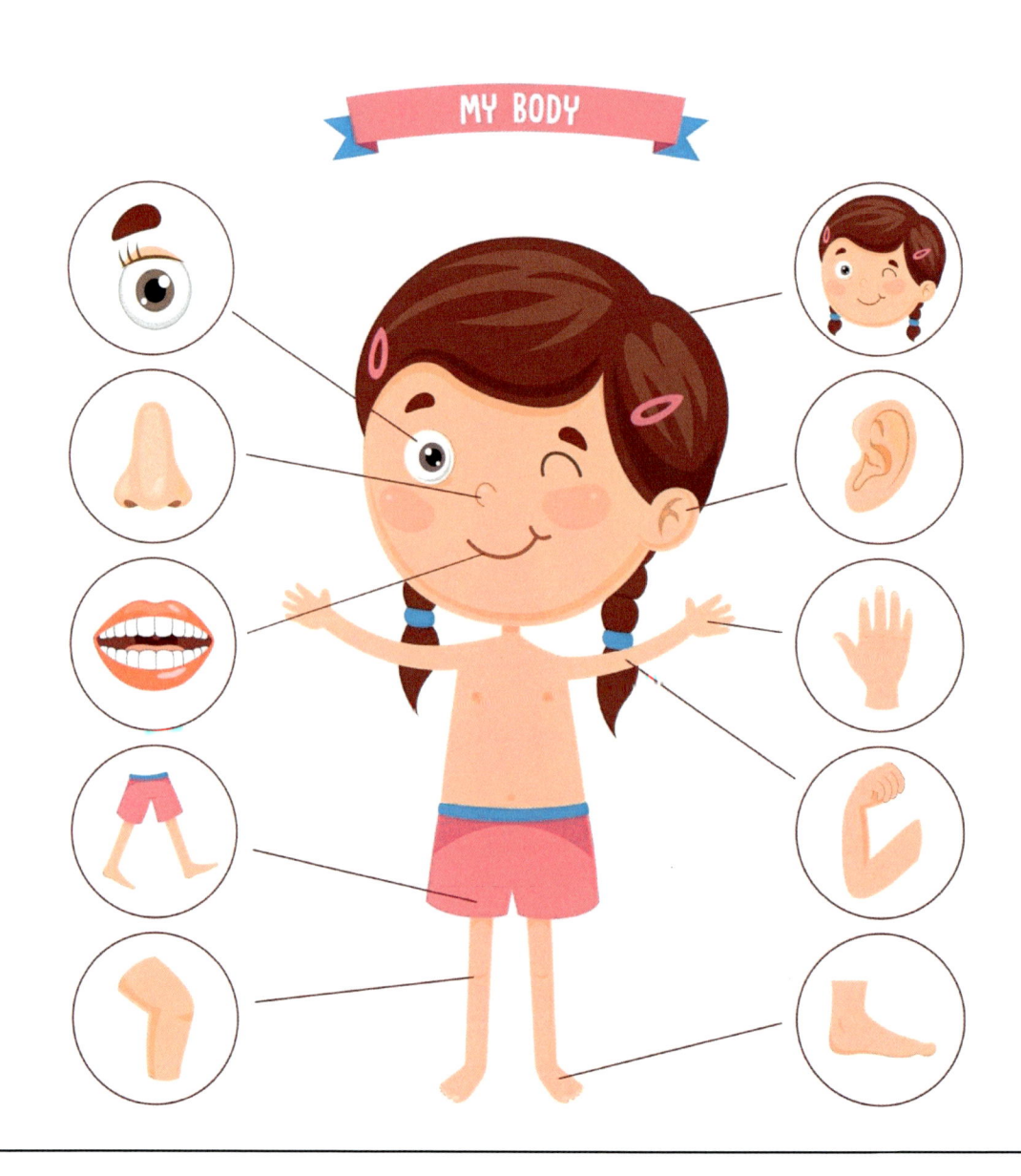

MY BODY

If we don't take care of our bodies, we can get sick. So, I scrub, scrub, scrub when I clean my body. I can take care of myself.

When my friends play and get really dirty, they don't want to take a bath.

But I know that keeping clean is part of loving me! So, I take a bath or a shower.

When I go potty, I use toilet paper to clean my bottom.

Then I wash my hands.

I wash them very carefully! I keep my hands clean. And, it keeps my family healthy, too! I can take care of myself!

WASH YOUR HANDS

1. WATER AND SOAP

2. PALM TO PALM

3. BETWEEN FINGERS

4. FOCUS ON THUMBS

5. BACK OF HANDS

6. FOCUS ON WHISTS

Sometimes, I even clip my nails!

One time I didn't eat enough vegetables and my tummy really hurt!

So the next time I saw vegetables, I ate them right up! Eating good food is a way to take care of myself!

Rae didn't brush her teeth. She got an awful toothache.

From then on, she brushed her teeth before she went to bed.

I brush my teeth. Clean teeth are healthy teeth! I can take care of myself!

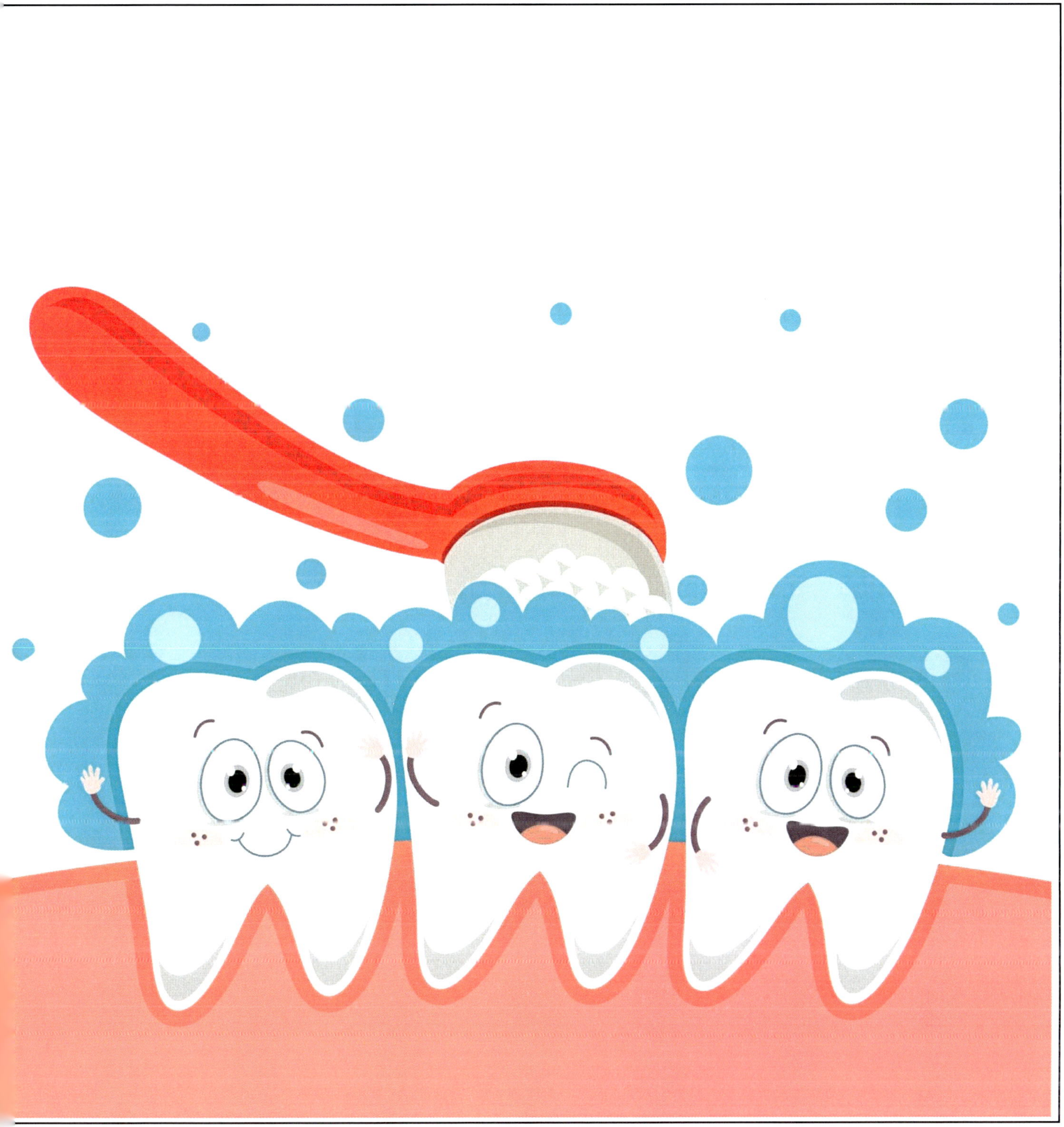

Sometimes I don't want to go to sleep. There are so many fun things to do! But I know if I get a good night's rest I will feel rested and strong in the morning. Sleeping well is a way I can take care of myself! (Even if my hair IS curly when I wake up!

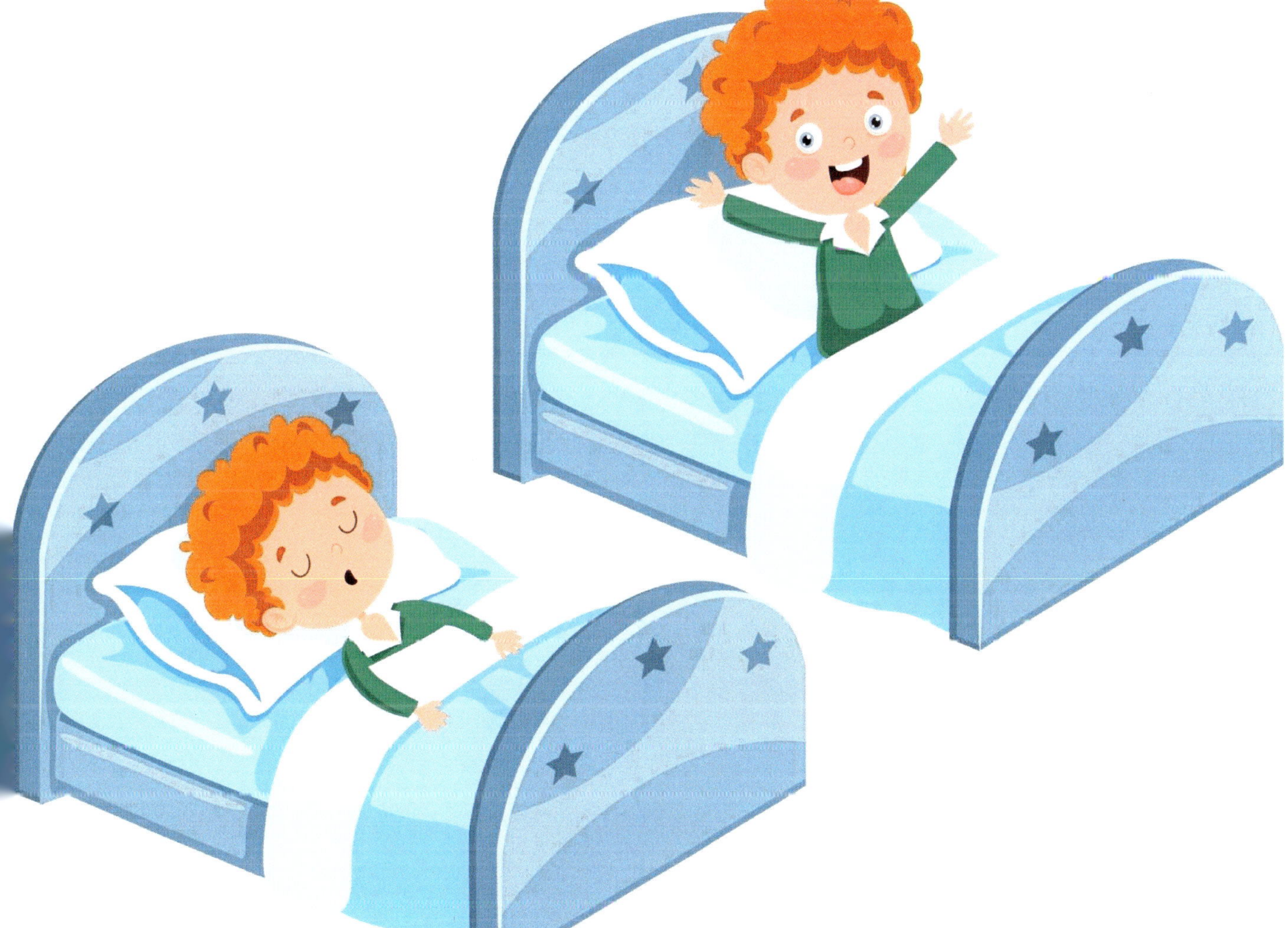

There are other things we can do, too! I love playing on the computer but…

I love basketball more!

When it's warm outside, I love playing outside in the sun. Sun is healthy! I don't like wearing the ooey gooey stuff on my skin but sunscreen keeps my skin healthy!

When it's cold outside, it's really important that I bundle up to stay warm! I can take care of myself!

One time I got sick. When I was sick, I stayed in bed. That's how I take care of myself!

I visit the doctor for checkups! I take care of myself!

My friend Izzy always covers her mouth when she sneezes. She takes care of her and me by using a tissue so I don't get sick!

Healthy or sick, I am very proud of me because I can take care of myself!

There are many other books by Andi Cann. Check them out at your favorite book seller!

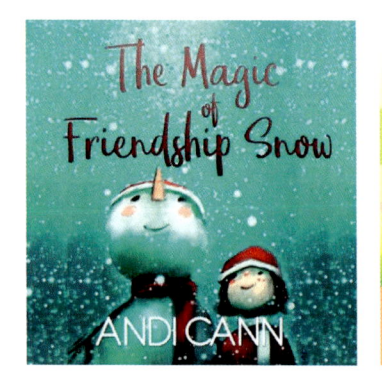

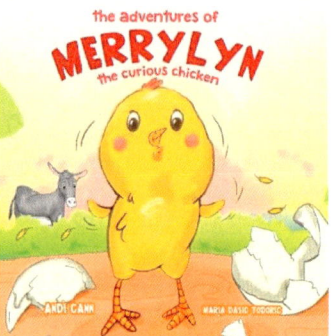

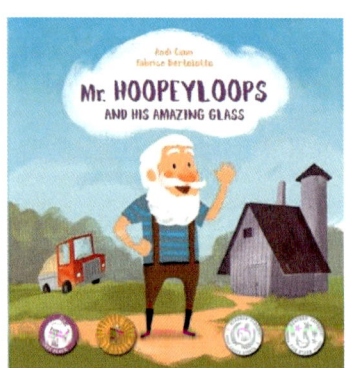

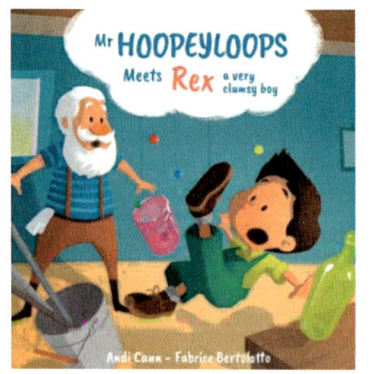

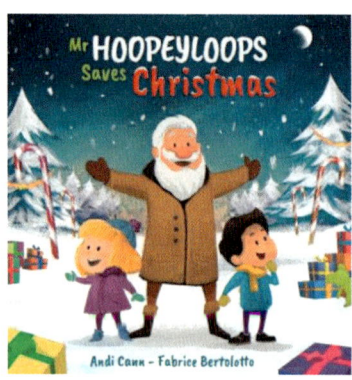

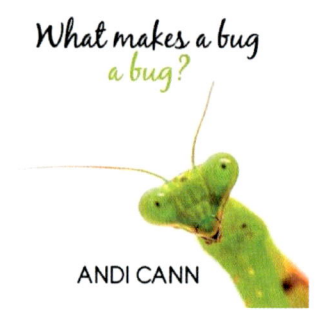

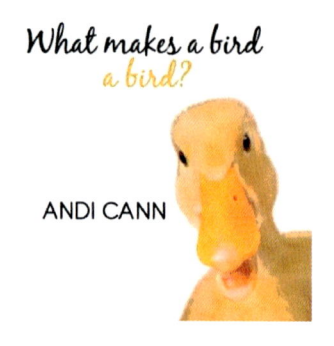

Please visit my website https://www.andicann.com and register your email address. You will receive a free book and be the first to know about new books, special offers, and free stuff!

If you have a chance, please write a review. It helps other readers and me, an independent author. Thank you!

Andi

This is a work of fiction. Names, characters, businesses, places, events, locales, and incidents are either the products of the author's imagination or used in a fictitious manner. Any resemblance to actual persons, living or dead, or actual events is purely coincidental.

We welcome you to include brief quotations in a review. If you would like to reproduce, store, or transmit the publication in whole or in part, please obtain written permission from the publisher. Otherwise, please do not store this publication in a retrieval system. Please do not transmit in any form or by any means electronic, mechanical, printing, photocopying, recording, or otherwise. Please honor our copyright! For permissions: Contact MindView Press via email: mindviewpress@gmail.com

Published by MindView Press: Hibou

ISBN-13:   978-1-949761-39-9   eBook
ISBN-13:   978-1-949761-40-5   Paperback
Copyright©2019 by Andrea L. Kamenca. All rights reserved.

Thank you for reading and for leaving a review!

Made in the USA
Las Vegas, NV
25 March 2025